# *Our* Washington, D.C.

WE HOLD THESE TRUTHS TO BE
EVIDENT: THAT ALL MEN ARE CR
EQUAL. THAT THEY ARE ENDOWED BY
CREATOR WITH CERTAIN INALIE
RIGHTS, AMONG THESE ARE LIFE, L
AND THE PURSUIT OF HAPPINESS
TO SECURE THESE RIGHTS GOVERN
ARE INSTITUTED AMONG MEN
SOLEMNLY PUBLISH AND DECLAR
THESE COLONIES ARE AND OF

**Voyageur Press**

Printed in China

04   05   06   07   08   5   4   3   2   1

Library of Congress Cataloging-in-Publication Data

Franklin, Paul M.
  Our Washington, D.C. / photography by Paul M. Franklin.
    p. cm.
  ISBN 0-89658-044-X (hardcover)
  1. Washington (D.C.)—Pictorial works.  I. Title.
  F195.F785 2004
  975.3'0022'2—dc22
                                    2003022805

Distributed in Canada by Raincoast Books,
9050 Shaughnessy Street, Vancouver, B.C. V6P 6E5

Published by Voyageur Press, Inc.
123 North Second Street, P.O. Box 338,
Stillwater, MN 55082 U.S.A.
651-430-2210, fax 651-430-2211
books@voyageurpress.com
www.voyageurpress.com

Page 1: *Cherry blossoms bloom near the United States Capitol.*

Page 2: *Fifty flags circle the base of the Washington Monument.*

Page 3, top: *The Tidal Basin bursts into flower during peak cherry blossoming.*

Page 3, bottom: *Visitors enjoy a historic mule-drawn boat ride on the C&O Canal.*

Page 4: *The National Christmas tree glows on the Ellipse outside the White House.*

Page 5: *Fireworks burst over the Mall.*

Title page: *The Jefferson Memorial overlooks the Tidal Basin.*

Title page inset: *Inside the Jefferson Memorial stands the statue of President Thomas Jefferson.*

Facing page: *Inspired by the principles of ancient Rome, the United States government built its Capitol to emulate Rome's Pantheon. The building also sits at the exact center of Washington, D. C. (Photograph © Tom Till)*

*A bird's-eye view of Washington, D. C. from an 1892 engraving by Currier & Ives showing the United States Capitol building in the center of the city.*

No Washington building may exceed the height of the Capitol, allowing the city's monuments to strike a bold contrast against the city's low-lying skyline.

Facing page: *Three of Washington's most enduring landmarks—The Lincoln Memorial, the Washington Monument, and the Capitol—glow in the night sky.*

Above: *An 1890s engraving of the Capitol by Currier & Ives showing the reconstructed dome after the British burned the building in the War of 1812.*

*The Capitol's central Rotunda features oil paintings, sculptures, and a frescoed frieze illustrating important events in American history. (Photograph © Jürgen Vogt)*

*This enormous canopy fresco covers the dome of the Capitol Rotunda. Painted by Italian-born artist Constantino Brumidi in 1865,* The Apotheosis of Washington *depicts President Washington ascending to the heavens. (Photograph © Mae Scanlon)*

*When designing the lovely grounds surrounding the Capitol, renowned landscape architect Frederick Law Olmsted positioned benches to offer the best views of the building. Other park features—minimal statues or ornamentation, for example—also respect the glory of the Capitol.*

Right: *Palm trees and other tropical flora soar in the grand, eighty-foot-tall Palm House, which serves as the focal point of the United States Botanic Garden's Conservatory. The palm leaf symbolizes victory and joy.*

Below: *The petite, themed gardens that comprise Bartholdi Park include the Romantic, Heritage, and Therapeutic Gardens.*

French sculptor Frédéric August Bartholdi created this cast-iron fountain for the Philadelphia International Exposition of 1876. Sea nymphs, tritons, and lighted globes adorn this elegant fountain, and represent the elements of water and light. Bartholdi would go on to sculpt the Statue of Liberty.

Established by Congress in 1820, the Botanic Garden houses a comprehensive orchid collection, including the exquisite Phaleanopsis, *also known as Ken's Speckled Delight.*

*Located in front of the Smithsonian Castle, the music and lights of the Carousel on the Mall draw weary visitors to this magical icon of Americana.*

Bottom: *Children love a spin on the Mall's antique merry-go-round.*

Top: *Carousel artists during the golden age of the merry-go-round hand-carved and painted the animals, such as this fantastical dragon "pony."*

*Against the stately backdrop of the National Gallery of Art's West Building, ice skaters glide on the Sculpture Garden's winter-time ice rink.*

Top: *The West Building of the National Gallery of Art exhibits an impressive collection of art from the thirteenth to the nineteenth centuries.*

Bottom: *The National Gallery of Art contains an extraordinary collection of impressionistic art by nineteenth-century French masters. Here, patrons view Renoir's* Oarsmen at Chateau *and Monet's* Artist's Garden Vetheuil.

Above: Typewriter Eraser, Scale X *by Claes Oldenburg and Coosje van Bruggen is one of twenty modern sculptures in the National Gallery of Art's spacious Sculpture Garden.*

Facing page: *The sharp angles and audacious asymmetry of the East Building make it perfect for housing the National Gallery of Art's modern collection, which includes pieces by Pablo Picasso, Henri Matisse, and Jackson Pollock. (Photograph © Mae Scanlon)*

*Children and parents alike flock to the National Museum of Natural History, which houses an astounding range of cultural artifacts. A cross-section includes a giant hissing cockroach and the Hope Diamond. (Photograph © Jürgen Vogt)*

Above: *The cylindrical Hirshhorn Museum exhibits one of the nation's best displays of modern art. Latvianborn Joseph Hirshhorn donated his personal collection to form the base of this museum's collection.*

Left: *Visitors to Hirshhorn Sculpture Garden view a provocative display of more than sixty contemporary sculptures, including bold, abstract works such as Auguste Rodin's headless* Walking Man.

*A central fountain, landscaped gardens, and park benches invite passersby to linger in front of the Smithsonian Institution's elegant Arts and Industries Building. (Photograph © Jürgen Vogt)*

*Oscar the Grouch is preserved as a cultural artifact in the National Museum of American History Sesame Street exhibit. (Photograph © Mae Scanlon)*

*You can almost hear Edith squalling, "Archie!" when viewing this* All in the Family *exhibit in the National Museum of American History. (Photograph © Mae Scanlon)*

*Sun warms the red sandstone walls of the Arts and Industries Building. Mary Livingston Ripley, wife of the Smithsonian Institution's eighth Secretary, conceived these gardens in 1978, thereby saving this now-gorgeous space from becoming a parking lot.*

Left: *A favorite with aviation enthusiasts, the National Air and Space Museum is chock-full of historic aircraft, including planes flown by Wilbur Wright, Charles Lindbergh, and Amelia Earhart. (Photograph © Jürgen Vogt)*

Above: *This undersize model resides in the Air and Space Museum. It is both a splendid representation of the Columbia Space Shuttle, and a sorrowful reminder of the events of February 1, 2003. (Photograph © Mae Scanlon)*

ONLY GUARD YOURSELF AND GUARD YOUR SOUL
CAREFULLY, LEST YOU FORGET THE THINGS YOUR
EYES SAW, AND LEST THESE THINGS DEPART
YOUR HEART ALL THE DAYS OF YOUR LIFE. AND YOU
SHALL MAKE THEM KNOWN TO YOUR CHILDREN,
AND TO YOUR CHILDREN'S CHILDREN.

DEUTERONOMY 4:9

HERE LIES EARTH GATHERED FROM DEATH CAMPS,
CONCENTRATION CAMPS, SITES OF MASS EXECUTION,
AND GHETTOS IN NAZI-OCCUPIED EUROPE, AND
FROM CEMETERIES OF AMERICAN SOLDIERS WHO
FOUGHT AND DIED TO DEFEAT NAZI GERMANY.

Above: *This eternal flame burns for the six million Jews, Romanies, homosexuals, and others systematically killed by the Third Reich. Open since 1993, the United States Holocaust Memorial Museum performs the vital task of keeping the atrocity of that genocide from receding into the forgotten remnants of history.*

Right: *Family portraits line the narrow walls of this deliberately claustrophobic Tower of Names exhibit in the Holocaust Memorial Museum.*

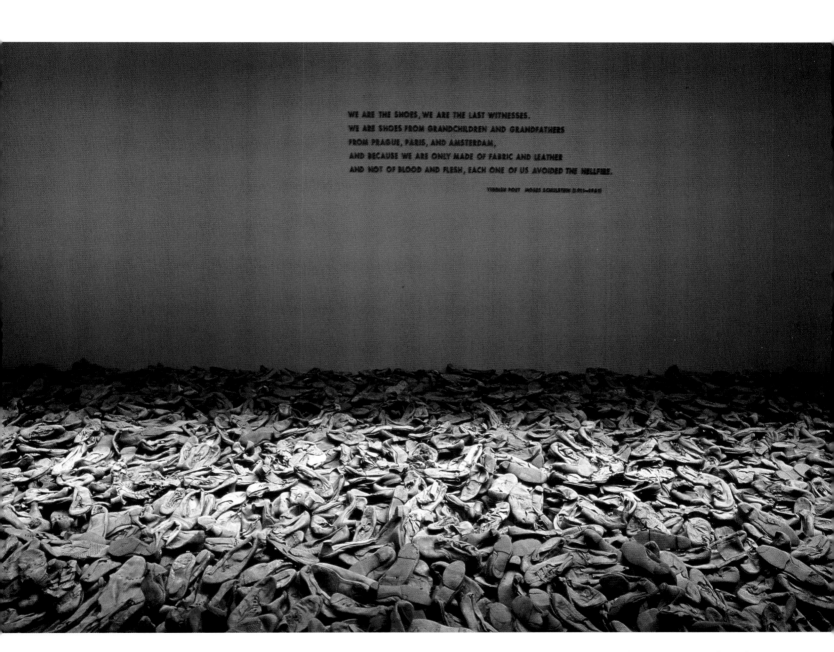

WE ARE THE SHOES, WE ARE THE LAST WITNESSES.
WE ARE SHOES FROM GRANDCHILDREN AND GRANDFATHERS
FROM PRAGUE, PARIS, AND AMSTERDAM,
AND BECAUSE WE ARE ONLY MADE OF FABRIC AND LEATHER
AND NOT OF BLOOD AND FLESH, EACH ONE OF US AVOIDED THE HELLFIRE.

YIDDISH POET   MOSES SCHULSTEIN (1911–1981)

*This simple, graphic exhibit in the Holocaust Memorial Museum displays shoes of the victims. The lines from Moses Schulstein's poem "I Saw a Mountain" bespeak the totality of destruction during the Holocaust.*

Left: *Americans past and present have gathered on the Mall in Washington to voice protest and support. Here, participants in the Million Mom March campaign for gun laws. The most famous assembly here was the 1963 March on Washington, when Dr. Martin Luther King, Jr. delivered his legendary "I Have a Dream" speech. (Photograph © Jürgen Vogt)*

Above: *This handmade memorial on F Street pleads for peace following the September 11 terrorist attacks, during which American Airlines Flight 77 crashed into the northwest side of the Pentagon.*

Facing page: *The Washington Monument soars over 550 feet into the sky. Fronted by Washington's famous cherry trees, this monolith memorializes our nation's first president and remains the most recognizable monument in the city.*

Left: *Engraving of the Washington Monument under construction. A large base colonnade was originally designed to encircle the monument, but was scratched from plans when funds ran short.*

Right: *A lovely spring night suddenly vanished while we viewed cherry blossoms.*
—*Japanese poet Basho (1644–1694)*

Below: *Washington's wondrous blossoming cherry trees were a gift from Japan. First Lady Helen Taft and Viscountess Chinda, wife of the Japanese ambassador, planted the first two trees in 1912. Nearly 200 of the original trees still bloom every spring in the Tidal Basin, inciting the annual Cherry Blossom Festival.*

*The Jefferson Memorial presides over the Tidal Basin. Within this neoclassical colonnade rests a bronze statue of the third president; the walls are engraved with lines from the Declaration of Independence.*

Left: *Wreaths ring the South Portico of the White House at Christmastime. United States presidents have lived in this 132-room mansion for over two centuries, though the British nearly burned it to the ground in the War of 1812; following their raid, a night of torrential rain checked the flames.*

Above: *Interior views of the White House's famous rooms from an 1860s engraving.*

Above: *This grand statue of President Andrew Jackson serves as the centerpiece of Lafayette Square. Formed from cannons Jackson acquired during the War of 1812, this statue overlooks the rear entry of the White House.*

Right: *Holiday garlands and sprays of greenery decorate the mantel and cascade from wall sconces in the State Dining Room. (Photograph courtesy the White House)*

Top: *The Red Room is decorated with garlands and topiaries made of pomegranates, pears, and magnolia leaves. A small cranberry tree surrounded by holly sits on an antique marble-top table. (Photograph courtesy the White House)*

Bottom: *Entrances to both the East Room and the State Dining Room from the Cross Hall are surrounded by garlands of pine cones, red glass balls, red icicles, and red pepper berries. (Photograph courtesy the White House)*

*One of the finest pieces of art in the White House, the portrait of Benjamin Franklin by David Martin is the centerpiece of the Green Room. (Photograph courtesy the White House)*

*A White House usher prepares the Blue Room for a luncheon. (Photograph courtesy the White House)*

President George W. Bush hosts a meeting on December 20, 2001, with senior advisers in the newly renovated Oval Office, which includes a specially designed wool rug featuring the Presidential Seal. The color scheme of the first Oval Office, built in 1909 during the Taft Administration, was olive green. (Photograph courtesy the White House)

Children race to reach the finish line by rolling hard-boiled eggs across the South Lawn of the White House during the annual White House Easter Egg Roll April 1, 2002. Honoring an Easter tradition that President Rutherford B. Hayes started in 1878, President George W. Bush and Mrs. Bush opened the peoples' home to children, games, and many rolling Easter eggs. (Photograph courtesy the White House)

Left: *Designed in the style of a Greek temple, the awe-inspiring Lincoln Memorial reflects into the luminous waters of the Reflecting Pool.*

Above: *Embodying President Abraham Lincoln's wise and tempered counsel, this seated statue is constructed of white Georgia marble and stands nineteen feet high. (Photograph © Gene Ahrens)*

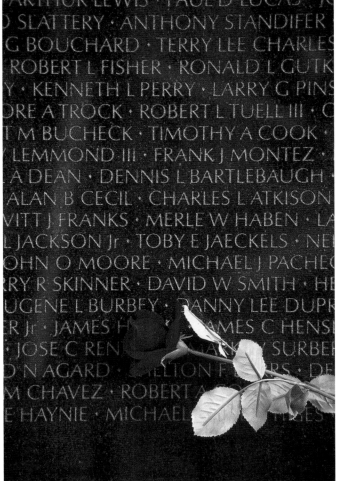

Left: *Low and dark, the Vietnam Veterans Memorial was initially condemned by some as a "black gash of shame." Two granite walls cut into the earth, one aiming toward the Lincoln Memorial, the other toward the Washington Monument. Understated but hardly irreverent, this unique memorial designed by twenty-one-year-old Yale student Maya Lin is now valued as one of the most moving monuments in Washington. (Photograph © Tom Till)*

Above: *Over 58,000 names are carved into the Vietnam Veterans Memorial. Visitors leave flowers, letters, pictures, and bring home crayon or charcoal rubbings of their loved one's name.*

Top: *Dedicated in 1993, the Vietnam Women's Memorial commemorates the female soldiers who aided in the war effort. Sculptor Glenna Goodacre created this bronze statue of women in uniform tending to an injured soldier.*

Bottom: *Nineteen soldiers patrol a field as part of the Korean War Veterans Memorial. These oversize stainless steel figures take on a ghostly feel as they stand in perpetual frozen motion, headed toward an American flag.*

*Two years after the construction of the Vietnam wall, the Veterans Memorial expanded to include this statue sculpted by Frederick Hart. The somber faces of the men serve as a realistic counterpart to the more abstract wall.*

*Anglers fish the waters in East Potomac Park. Visitors to this 328-acre park can also golf, play tennis, swim, or enjoy a picnic under the cherry trees.*

*This fearsome sculpture rises from Hains Point in East Potomac Park. In truth,* The Awakening *is one of the most delightful landmarks in Washington. Cast in aluminum by sculptor J. Seward Johnson, Jr., this giant has allowed legions of children to scale his emerging body parts.*

Top: *These charming Victorian-style row houses belong to Washington's oldest residential neighborhood, Capitol Hill.*

Bottom: *A Sunday stroll through Capitol Hill rewards visitors with Eastern Market's outdoor flea market, where vendors display a tempting assortment of flowers, jewelry, antiques, and other curios.*

*Eastern Market's block-long hall, standing since 1871, hosts the Market Lunch amidst the pungent aroma of roasted chicken and baking bread. The market sells a hearty assortment of meats, cheeses, and breads, as well as Old World wares such as pigs' feet.*

*The Canine Club tour poses in front of Doolittle's pet supply store, one of many small shops located near Eastern Market.*

*The Georgetown Flea Market on Wisconsin Avenue invites pedestrians to stroll through streets laden with artwork.*

*Dog lovers head to Capitol Hill on Saturday to sample the produce at Eastern Market's canine-friendly farmers' market.*

Above: *The Library of Congress's magnificent Thomas Jefferson Building emulates the ornate design of the Paris Opera House. After fire destroyed the original collection in 1814, Jefferson replenished the materials with his personal library of 6,487 books. (Photograph © Mae Scanlon)*

Facing page: *The domed Main Reading Room gains first-time researchers access to the Library of Congress's massive collection of books, maps, photographs, sheet music, and more. Above the mahogany reading desks perch ten-foot-high statues that embody the characteristics of human enterprise. (Photograph © Jürgen Vogt)*

Facing page: *Autumn heralds the convening of the United States Supreme Court. On the first Monday in October, the justices assemble in this temple-like building. Historic cases settled here include* Brown v. Board of Education *and* Roe v. Wade. *(Photograph © Scott T. Smith)*

Top: *Built in 1801, the Octagon temporarily accommodated President and First Lady Madison after the British burned the White House in the War of 1812. The recently renovated Octagon now houses the Museum of the American Architectural Foundation. (Photograph © Mae Scanlon)*

Bottom: *The Octagon hosts exhibits on architecture and Washington history, including this Treaty Room exhibit. In this second-floor study, President James Madison signed the Treaty of Ghent, ending the War of 1812. (Photograph © Mae Scanlon)*

On April 14, 1865, this small theater witnessed the assassination of President Abraham Lincoln. Theatergoers balked at returning to this tragic site, and owner John Ford was soon forced to sell. Over a century later, the government returned Ford's Theatre to its former resplendence. The Presidential Box, stage left, bears the constant mark of honor to the fallen president. (Photograph © Tom Till)

Left: *President Franklin Roosevelt, who contracted polio at the age of thirty-nine, led the country from a wheelchair, though few Americans were aware of his disability. Fittingly, the seven-and-a-half-acre Franklin Delano Roosevelt Memorial has been handicapped accessible since its dedication in 1997.*

Below: *Franklin Delano Roosevelt served as president from 1933 to 1945, including the heart of the Great Depression. This sculpture, Breadline, in the Franklin Delano Roosevelt Memorial depicts one of the many breadlines that marked this era in America.*

Above: *This statue pays tribute to George Mason, the founding father who, in 1787, refused to sign the United States Constitution because it did not sufficiently protect the individual from the government. In 1791, due in large part to Mason's steadfast campaign, the Bill of Rights was added to the U.S. Constitution.*

Right: *First occupied in 1824 by the United States' original Surgeon General, the Blair House now accommodates visiting dignitaries during their stay in Washington. (Photograph © Mae Scanlon)*

Facing page: *Many presidents have worshipped in St. John's Episcopal Church in Lafayette Park, leading it to be dubbed the Church of the Presidents. (Photograph © Mae Scanlon)*

Above: *Foreign flags fly over Embassy Row on Massachusetts Avenue. Formerly the residences of Washington's most affluent families, many of these homes were sold to foreign ambassadors during the Depression.*

Right: *The enormous Basilica of the National Shrine of the Immaculate Conception combines Romanesque and Byzantine styles. With more than 200 stained glass windows and the space to seat over 6,000 worshippers, it is the largest Catholic church in America. (Photograph © Mae Scanlon)*

A burglarproof vault and a marble Cash Room still reside in the Treasury Building, where United States currency was printed between 1863 and 1880. This Greek Revival building now houses the U.S. Treasury Department. (Photograph © Mae Scanlon)

Washington's architectural wonders extended underground with the 1976 construction of the Metrorail. Efficiently ferrying millions of visitors and government workers each year, the clean and easy-to-use Metro beats sweating through rush hour traffic or circling for the city's limited parking spaces. (Photograph © Jürgen Vogt)

Pedestrians stroll past the historic Internal Revenue Service Building. Built in eighteenth-century French Renaissance style, the IRS Building serves as a graceful transition between surrounding buildings of various architectural styles. (Photograph © Mae Scanlon)

Tulips bloom near the Old Post Office, a twelve-story Romanesque building that many once felt clashed with Washington's largely neoclassical design. Saved from demolition by preservationists, the building now houses the Old Post Office Pavilion, complete with restaurants and shops. (Photograph © Mae Scanlon)

*Visitors linger in Dupont Circle, a small park bounded by Connecticut, Massachusetts, and New Hampshire Avenues. The centerpiece of this park is the Francis Dupont Memorial Fountain, named for a Civil War admiral. The marble fountain's figures symbolize the sea, the wind, the stars, and the navigational arts.*

*A thriving diversity of cultures makes up the hip Adams-Morgan neighborhood, where sidewalk cafés and bohemian shops abound. Christened during the 1950s civil rights movement, Adams-Morgan pairs the names of two previously segregated schools—the white Adams School and the black Morgan School.*

The gorgeous architecture of Adams-Morgan reflects its nineteenth- and early-twentieth-century heritage. Below these colorful row houses and apartment buildings thrive a panoply of ethnic restaurants, bookstores, antique shops, palm readers, and sidewalk vendors selling everything from sneakers and watches to hand-made jewelry.

Adams-Morgan becomes a sidewalk community during Washington's relentlessly hot summer. Because the neighborhood sits at a higher elevation than the rest of the city, a welcome breeze often cools the throngs of outdoor patrons.

Right: *In the 1880s, Washington kept live animals on the Mall, where they were studied as taxidermists' models. Today, the National Zoo is world-renowned for its commitment to natural environments, conservation, and breeding programs. Here, a captivity-bred giraffe calf stays close to its mother's side.*

Below: *Soccer players compete in Anacostia Park. The 1,200-acre park also contains facilities for golf, tennis, basketball, rollerblading, and boating.*

Facing page: *In 2001, the National Zoological Park welcomed giant pandas Tian Tian and Mei Xiang. Here, one of the pair lounges amidst the green grasses native to its natural habitat.*

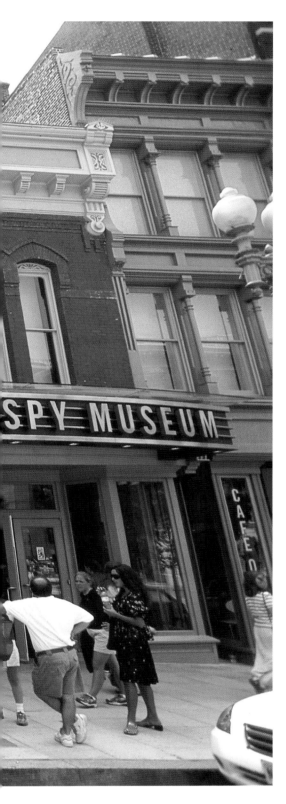

Left: *The International Spy Museum draws visitors to its fascinating exhibits on topics such as spying in biblical times and Cold War spy techniques.*

Above: *The arrival of professional basketball and hockey helped to revitalize this section of downtown Washington. The MCI Center, opened in 1997, also hosts the circus, concerts, and ice-skating exhibitions.*

*Visitors toss pennies into Columbus Memorial Fountain in front of Union Station. Modeled after the famous Roman Baths of Diocletian, this grand station was the largest in the world when it opened in 1908.*

*Gilded with gold leaf during an extensive 1988 renovation, Union Station's glorious barrel-vaulted ceiling soars ninety-six feet above café patrons.*

Top: *Muslim men and women pray at the Islamic Mosque and Cultural Center five times a day. Located on Massachusetts Avenue, the center features a minaret and sumptuous Persian rugs.*

Bottom: *This bronze statue of Albert Einstein sits in front of the National Academy of Sciences, a non-profit organization that brings the latest scientific discoveries to the American public. Sculpted in mashed-potato style, Robert Berks's statue pays tribute to the great physicist, who joined the Academy in 1942.*

*History was made at this complex on the night of June 17, 1972, when burglars were caught breaking into Democratic National Committee headquarters. Facing impeachment for his involvement in the Watergate scandal, Richard Nixon resigned his office of presidency two years later. (Photograph © Jürgen Vogt)*

Facing page: *Students at Georgetown University lunch below the Gothic towers of Healy Hall. The oldest Catholic college in the nation, Georgetown University boasts a beautiful campus. (Photograph © Mae Scanlon)*

Above: *Colorful townhouses and shady trees line the narrow cobblestone streets that wind through trendy Georgetown.*

Above: *Nestled amidst well-kept perennial and fruit tree gardens, Georgetown's Old Stone House preserves the past. This 1765 fieldstone cottage pre-dates the American Revolution and is, by some accounts, the oldest house in Washington.*

Right: *Once functioning as an essential part of Georgetown's booming milling industry, the now-peaceful Chesapeake and Ohio Canal is protected as a national park.*

*A mule-drawn canal clipper drifts down the C&O Canal. During the spring and summer months, park rangers guide these boat trips on the historic waterway.*

Top: *Once bustling with mules during the heyday of the C&O Canal, these shady towpaths now provide sanctuary to artists and cyclists alike.*

Bottom: *An outdoorsman kayaks a tranquil stretch of the C&O Canal.*

Above: *The Great Falls Tavern doubles as a history center for the C&O Canal and a magnificent viewing point of the roaring falls. (Photograph © Mae Scanlon)*

Facing page: *Boats dock at Washington Harbor, a six-acre riverfront development that encompasses restaurants, shops, offices, and condominiums.*

Left: *Stone terraces create a series of cozy enclaves in this sprawling ten-acre garden. Landscaped in 1920 by Beatrix Farrand, Dumbarton Oaks encompasses traditional English, Italian, and French gardens.*

Above: *Winding brick paths and fragrant blooms invite visitors to wander through the formal rose garden of Georgetown's Dumbarton Oaks.*

*The towering Church of Saint Peter and Saint Paul represents fourteenth-century Gothic architecture, complete with flying buttresses and stone gargoyles. Better known as the Washington National Cathedral, this church contains the tomb of President Woodrow Wilson.*

*The Bishop's Garden covers the grounds outside the National Cathedral. This English-style garden hosts a lush array of tea roses, yew trees, and other plants set amidst European stonework.*

Top: *This Georgian mansion sits on a twentyfive-acre estate that formerly belonged to Post cereal heir and art collector Majorie Merriweather Post. Opened to the public in 1977, Hillwood Museum exhibits Post's personal collection of Russian and French art from the eighteenth and nineteenth centuries.*

Bottom: *Azaleas flourish amidst the curving walkways and the dense woods of Hillwood Gardens.*

Facing page: *A series of streams, ponds, and wooden bridges interlace in Hillwood Gardens' peaceful Japanese-style garden, landscaped during the 1950s rise of American interest in Japanese culture.*

Facing page: *A family enjoys the impressive flowering azaleas in the United States National Arboretum.*

Above: *Evergreens surround a pagoda in the National Arboretum. The Japanese Garden also features a collection of bonsai, with some trees as old as 380 years.*

*Fall's chilly days turn leaves in the National Arboretum into a gorgeous tapestry of autumn colors. The arboretum's varied plantings make it a year-round haven.*

Top: *Morning sun encourages Egyptian lotuses to open in Kenilworth Aquatic Gardens. This wetland sanctuary also harbors water lilies and hyacinths.*

Bottom: *Columns jut into the air above a bluff in the National Arboretum. These pillars formerly stood in the United States Capitol building.*

*A golfer takes a practice swing on Rock Creek Park's eighteen-hole course.*

*The waters of Rock Creek flow through the now-inoperable Pierce Mill. Built in the 1820s, this historic gristmill operated as recently as 1993.*

Facing page: *Visitors to Rock Creek Park rest near a small waterfall. The creek runs the length of the 1,800-acre park, from the Lincoln Memorial to the Maryland border.*

Above: *Outdoor cafés line the streets of Bethesda, Maryland, where urban growth has spurred a lively restaurant scene.*

Facing page: *Café patrons relax outside Bethesda Row Cinema. This art house theatre offers amenities such as stadium seating and an espresso bar, along with provocative independent films.*

Facing page: *The Pentagon's concrete façade serves as an impressive backdrop to the Columbia Island Marina.*

Above: *A modern skyscraper in downtown Arlington, Virginia, dominates the skyline.*

Above: *This soldier guards the Tomb of the Unknowns in Virginia's Arlington National Cemetery. His precise and somber sentry represents the nation's respect for the thousands of slain American soldiers who remain unidentified. (Photograph © Mae Scanlon)*

Right: *The Japanese island of Iwo Jima witnessed one of the most terrible battles of World War II. Photographer Joe Rosenthal captured the image of five Marines and a Navy Corpsman raising the American flag; sculptor Felix DeWeldon later translated the image into this reverent statue, dedicated in 1954.*

*A couple walks a nature trail in Theodore Roosevelt Island. Two and a half miles of trails run through this island dedicated to President Roosevelt, an outdoorsman and conservationist.*

Above: *The Filene Center hosts outdoor performances of music and dance in Wolf Trap Farm Park. A national park in Vienna, Virginia, Wolf Trap hosts a wonderful range of rock, pop, chamber, opera, jazz, country, and folk concerts, as well as ballet and Broadway musicals.*

Left: *Concert-goers picnic on the Wolf Trap lawn in the summer months. The center's world-famous performers draw large, enthusiastic crowds.*

Above: *The modest, weathered exterior of Gadsby's Tavern belies the grandeur of this hostelry's past. Now a museum, this historic tavern in Alexandria, Virginia, was once a hotbed of political and social activity; George Washington even celebrated a birthday here.*

Facing page: *This graceful home in Glen Echo, Maryland, once housed Clara Barton, the woman who organized the American Red Cross in 1881.*

Left: *George Washington lived in this home in Virginia for forty-five years. Under Washington's supervision, Mount Vernon transformed from a modest farmhouse into the elegant manor pictured here.*

Above: *Mount Vernon's 500-acre estate contains several gardens and a greenhouse. The Upper Garden grows flowers, the Lower Garden vegetables and berries.*

*Mount Vernon's historically mindful Upper Garden blooms with the same flower and plant species that President Washington enjoyed in the late eighteenth century.*

Left: *Before becoming a military and political leader, George Washington was a yeoman farmer. A tour of the Mount Vernon estate reveals many historical farming techniques, some pioneered by Washington himself. Here, a woman demonstrates wool carding.*

Below: *Visitors view Mount Vernon's Pioneer Farm from the comfort of an old-fashioned horse-drawn wagon. Behind them is Washington's unusual sixteen-sided treading barn.*

*This memorial marks the burial ground of George Washington's many slaves. It was erected in 1983 with the backing of the NAACP and the local African American community. The central column symbolizes the strength of the enslaved; the three circles symbolize the source of their strength—faith, hope, and love. (Photograph © Mae Scanlon)*